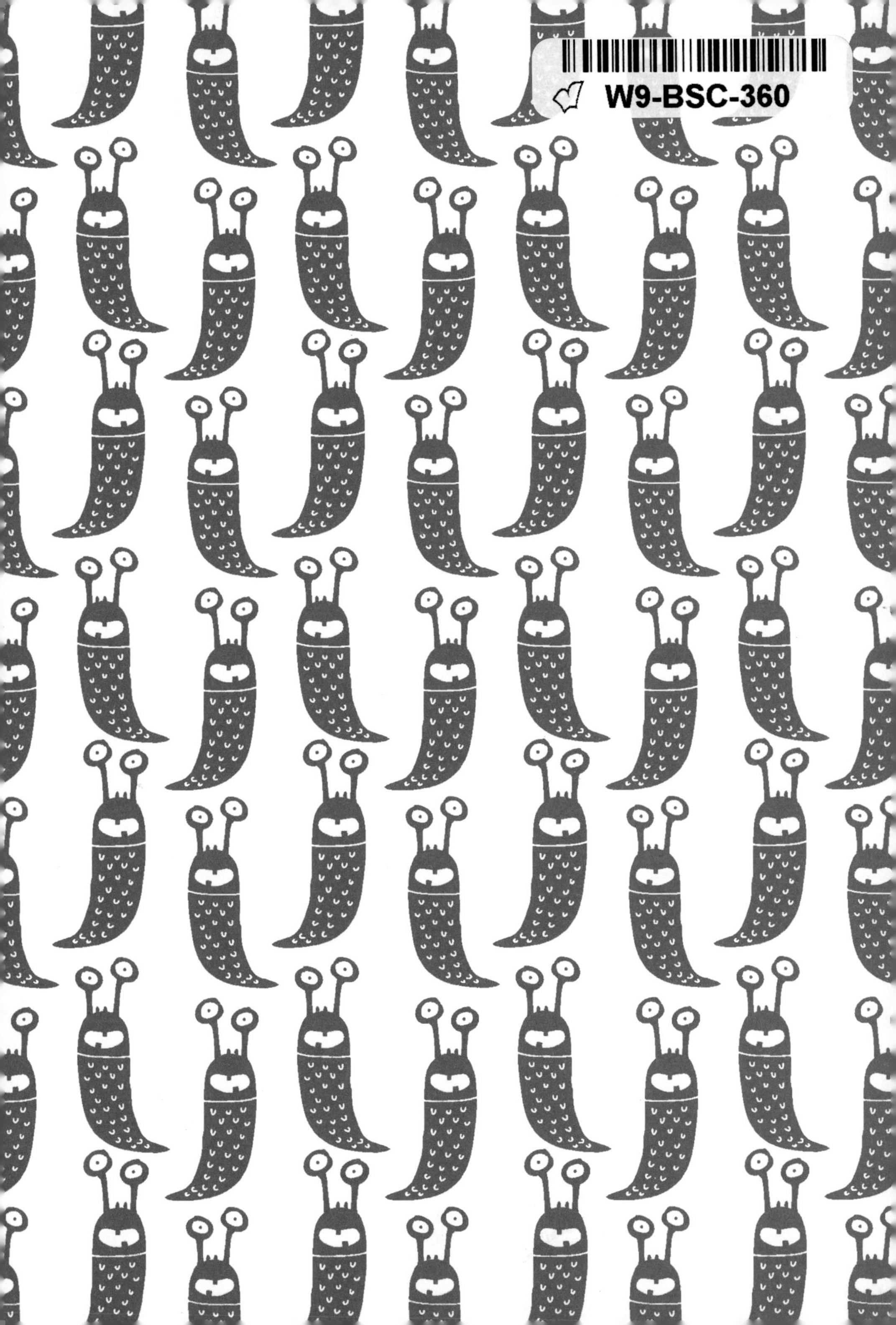

THE SLUG

For Henri,
but only when he has a cold

Originally published as *La limace* by Les éditions de la courte échelle inc.

Copyright © 2014 Elise Gravel
Copyright for the French edition: Elise Gravel and Les éditions de la courte échelle inc., 2013

Published in Canada by Tundra Books, a division of Random House of Canada Limited,
One Toronto Street, Suite 300, Toronto, Ontario M5C 2V6

Published in the United States by Tundra Books of Northern New York,
P.O. Box 1030, Plattsburgh, New York 12901

Library of Congress Control Number: 2013953638

Library and Archives Canada Cataloguing in Publication

Gravel, Elise
[Limace. English]
       The slug / by Elise Gravel.

(Disgusting critters)
Translation of: La limace.
Issued in print and electronic formats.
ISBN 978-1-77049-655-2 (bound).—ISBN 978-1-77049-657-6 (epub)

       I. Slugs (Mollusks)—Juvenile literature. I. Title. II. Title: Limace. English

QL430.4 G7213 2014   j594'.3   C2013-907508-9
                                       C2013-907509-7

English edition edited by Samantha Swenson
Designed by Elise Gravel and Tundra Books
The artwork in this book was rendered digitally.

www.tundrabooks.com

Printed and bound in China

1 2 3 4 5 6   19 18 17 16 15 14

Elise Gravel

THE SLUG

TITLE I

Tundra Books

Ladies and gentlemen, let me introduce

THE SLUG.

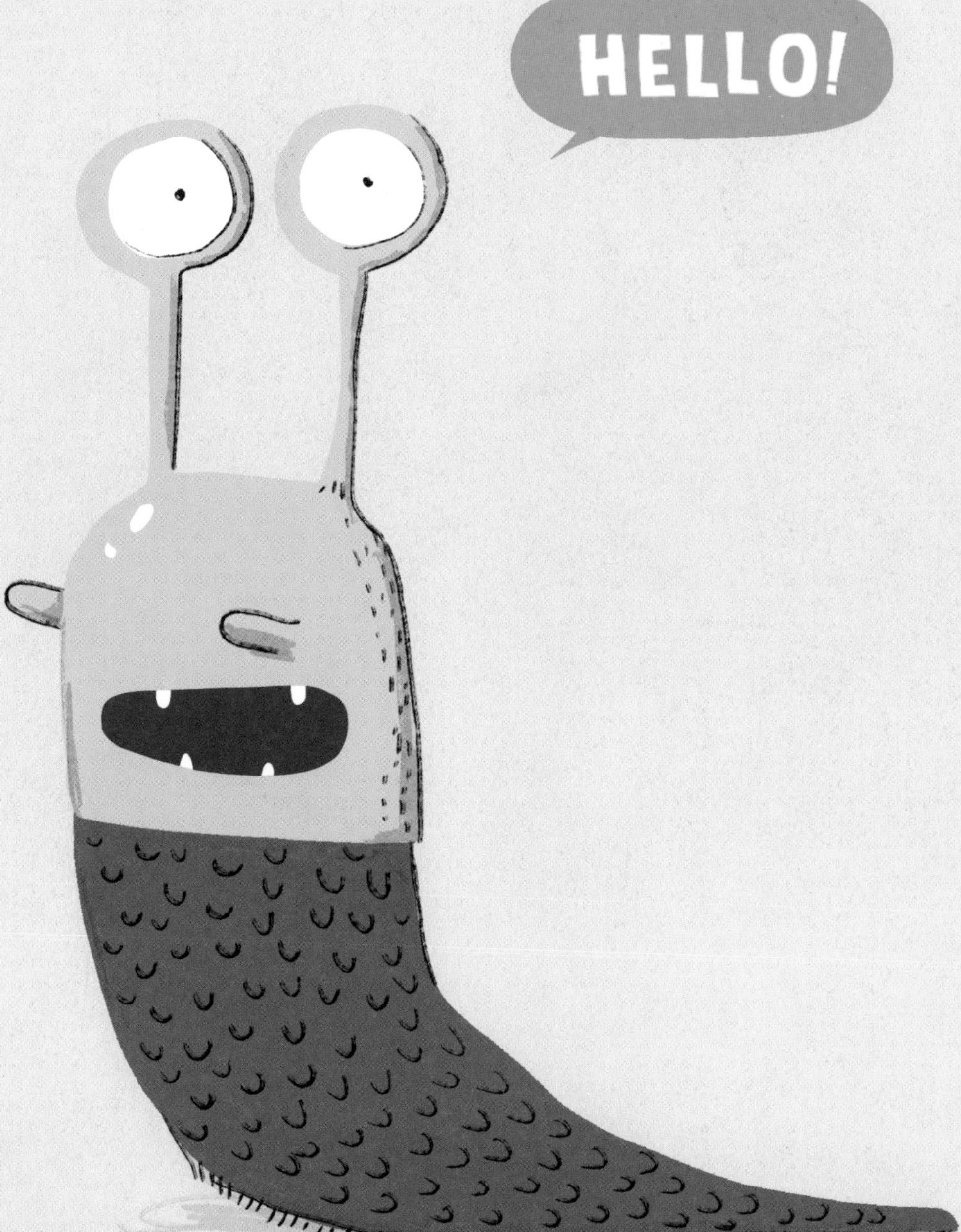
HELLO!

The slug is a mollusk, like the snail, but it doesn't have a

SHELL.

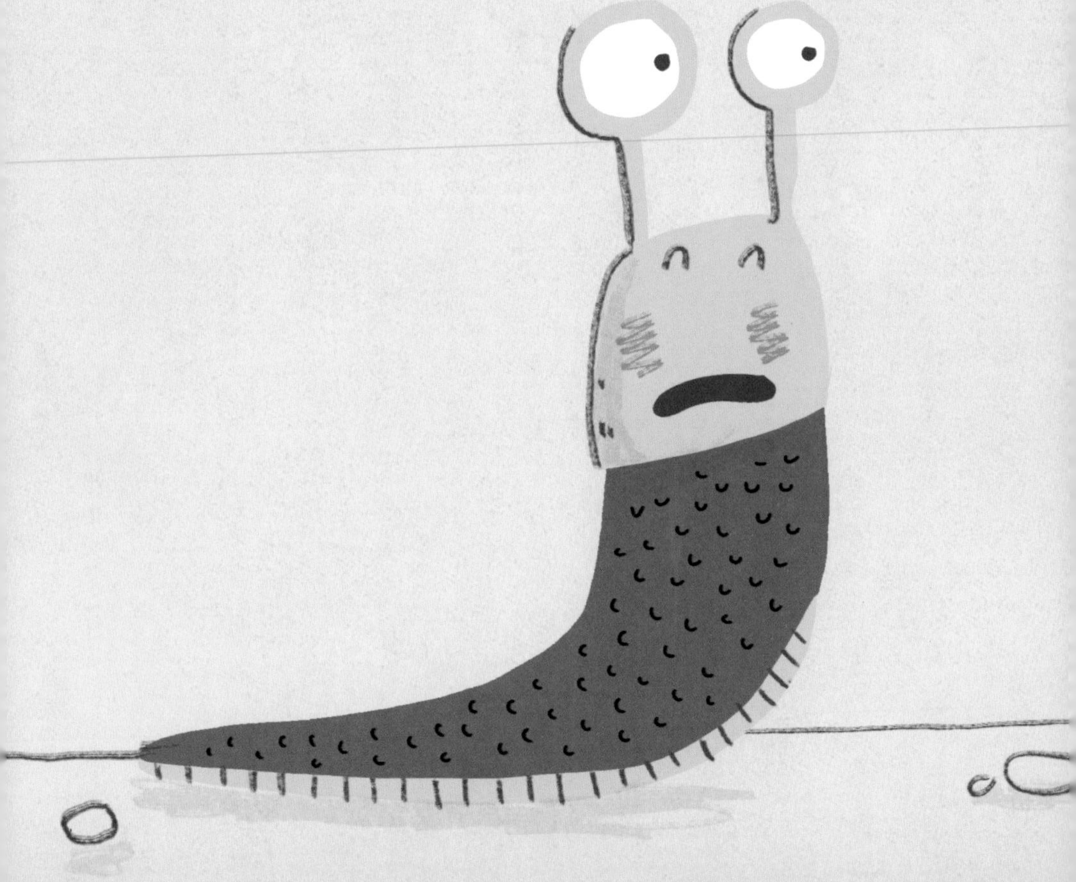

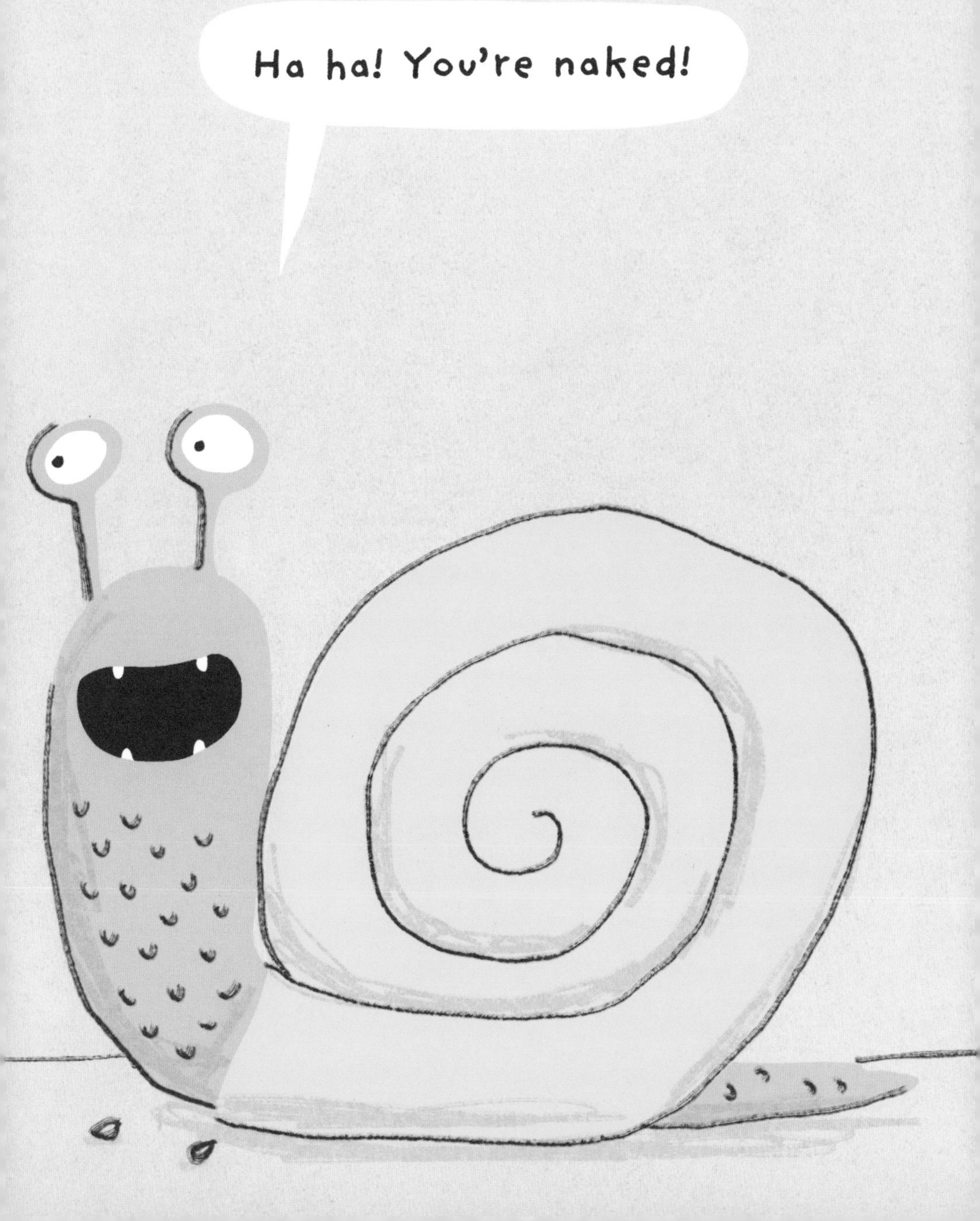
Ha ha! You're naked!

There are

MANY SPECIES

of slugs.

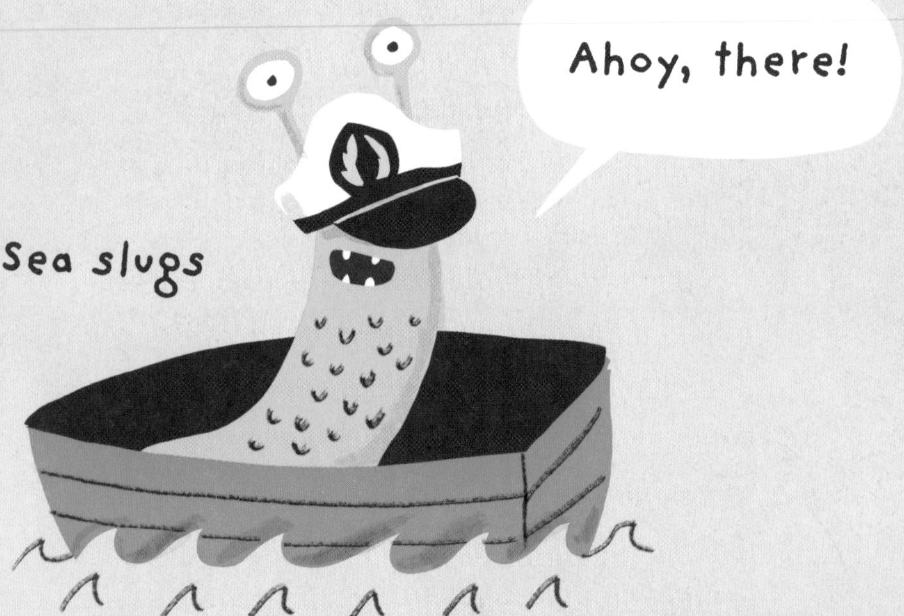
Ahoy, there!

Sea slugs

Rub-a-dub-dub,
one slug in a tub.

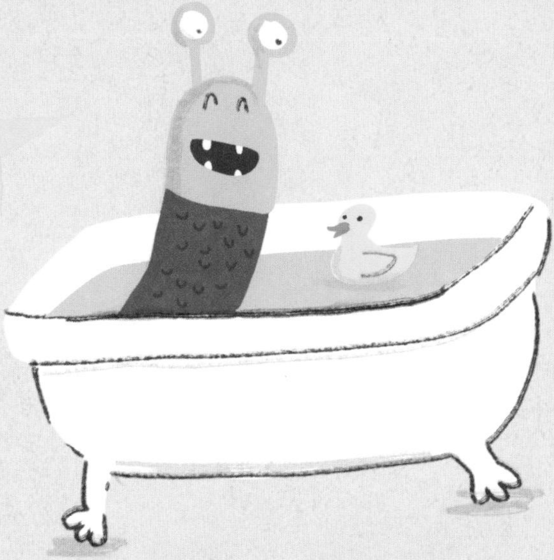

Freshwater slugs

Land slugs

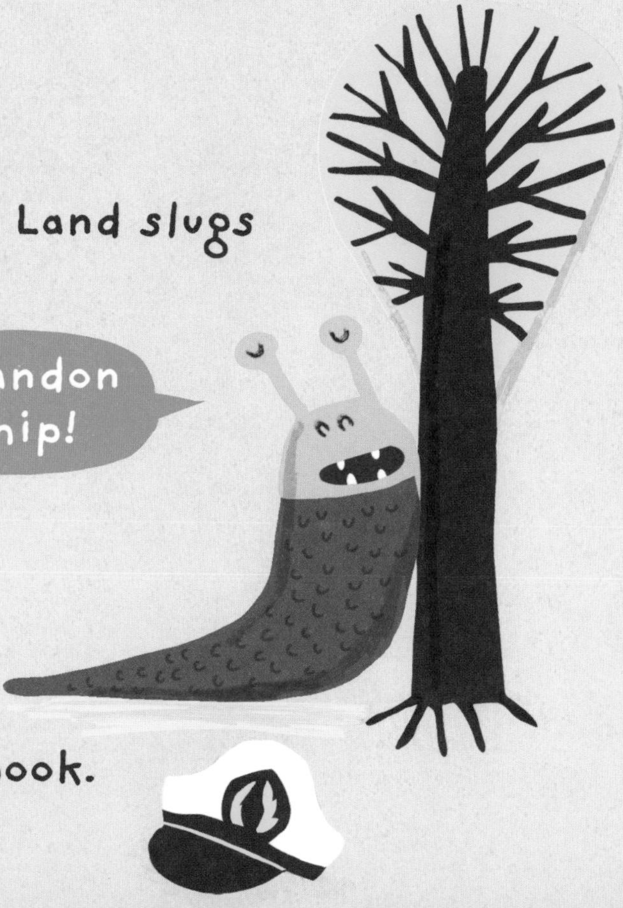
Abandon ship!

Land slugs are the ones we'll talk about in this book.

The slug has two pairs of

TENTACLES

on its head. The upper ones are eyes, and the lower ones are for smelling and tasting.

I see you! You're a kid and you smell like broccoli!

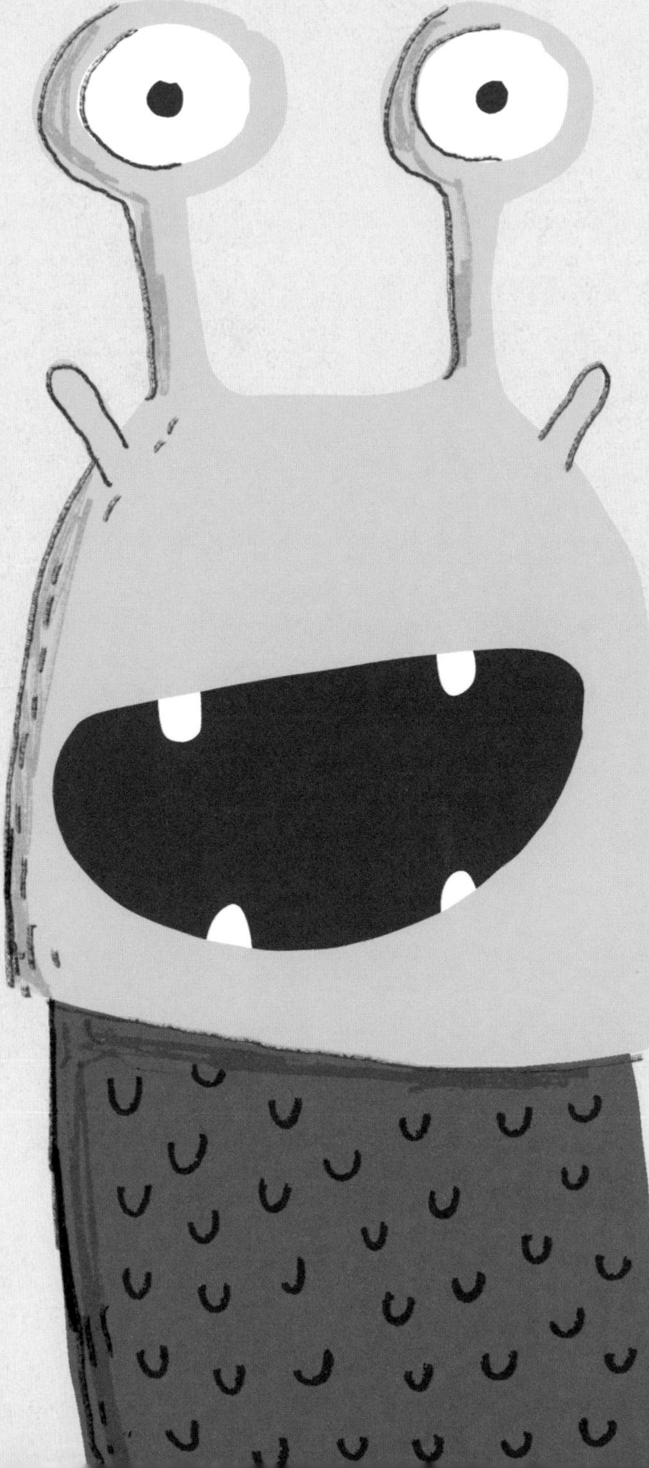

Its tentacles are

RETRACTABLE,

which means that the slug can pull them
inside its head when it senses

DANGER.

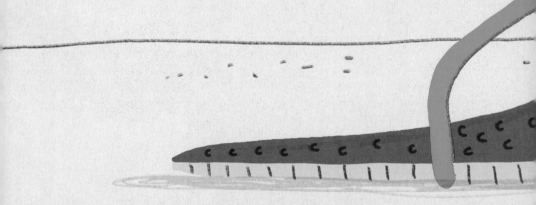

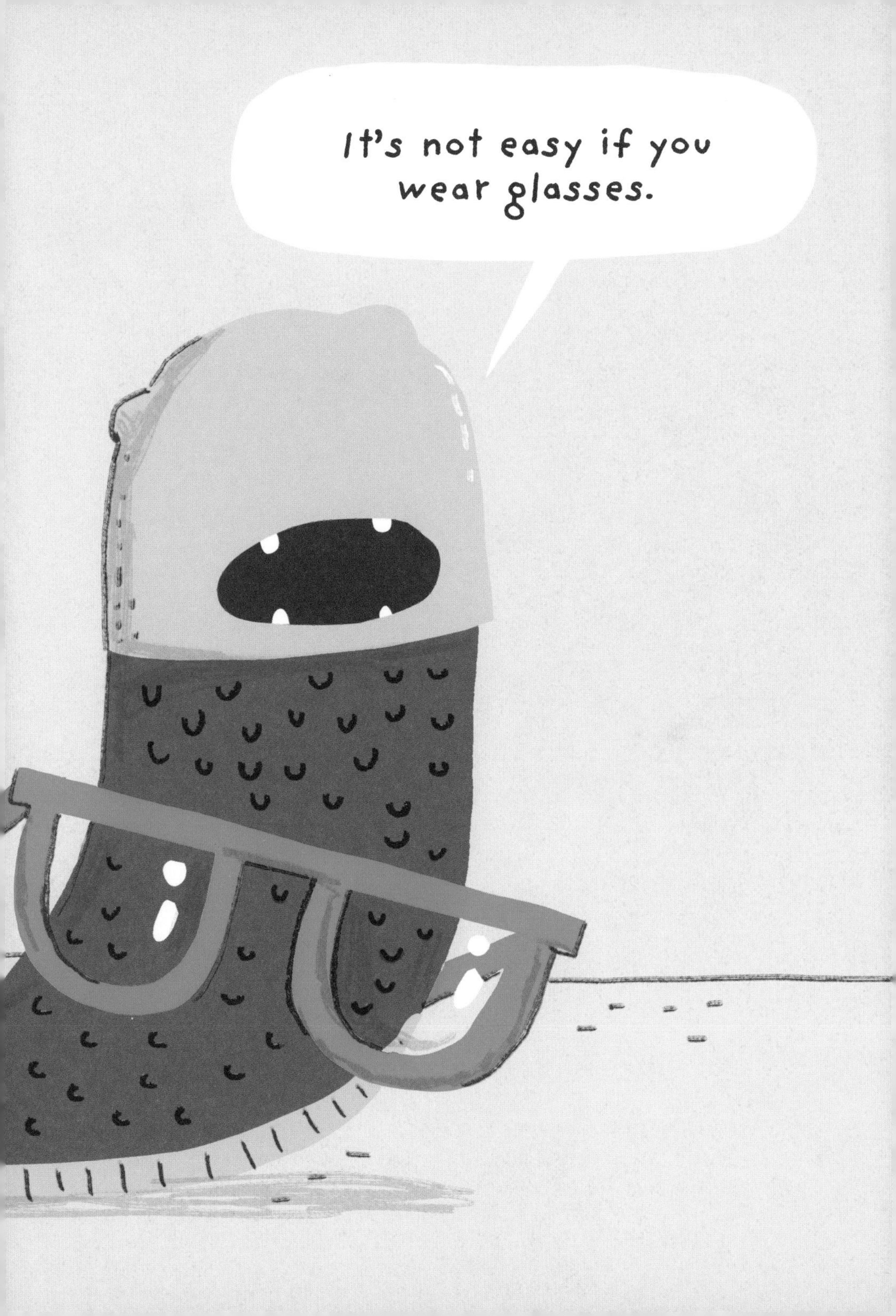
It's not easy if you wear glasses.

The slug

BREATHES

through a hole on the side of its body.

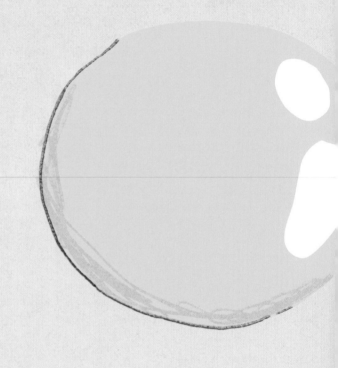
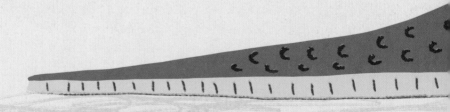

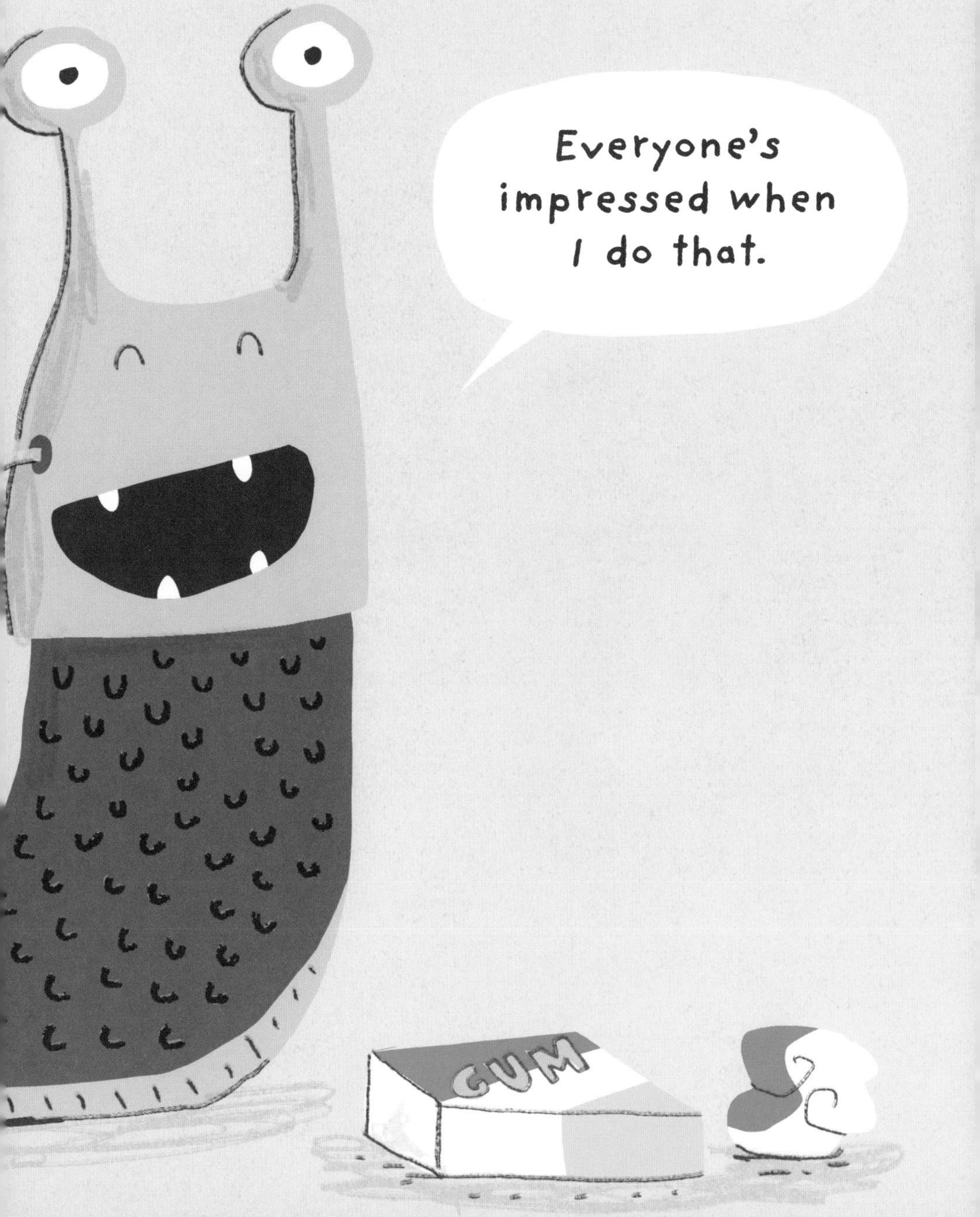
Everyone's impressed when I do that.

The slug

MOVES

by contracting the muscles
on its belly. Its belly is called a

FOOT.

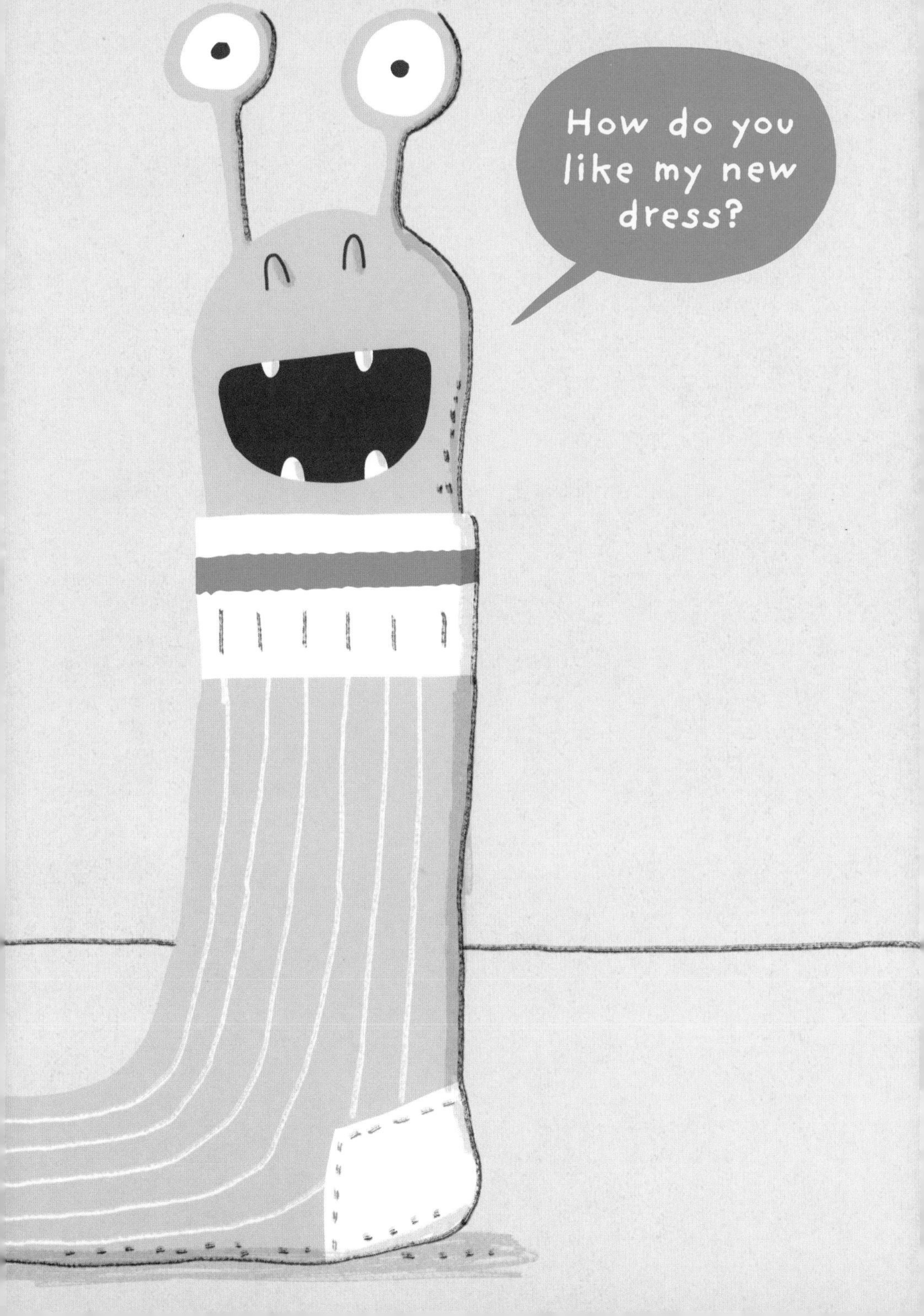
How do you like my new dress?

The slug's whole body is covered in

a thick and slimy liquid (kind of like snot!). It has to stay in humid areas, such as under stones or flower pots, so it doesn't dry out.

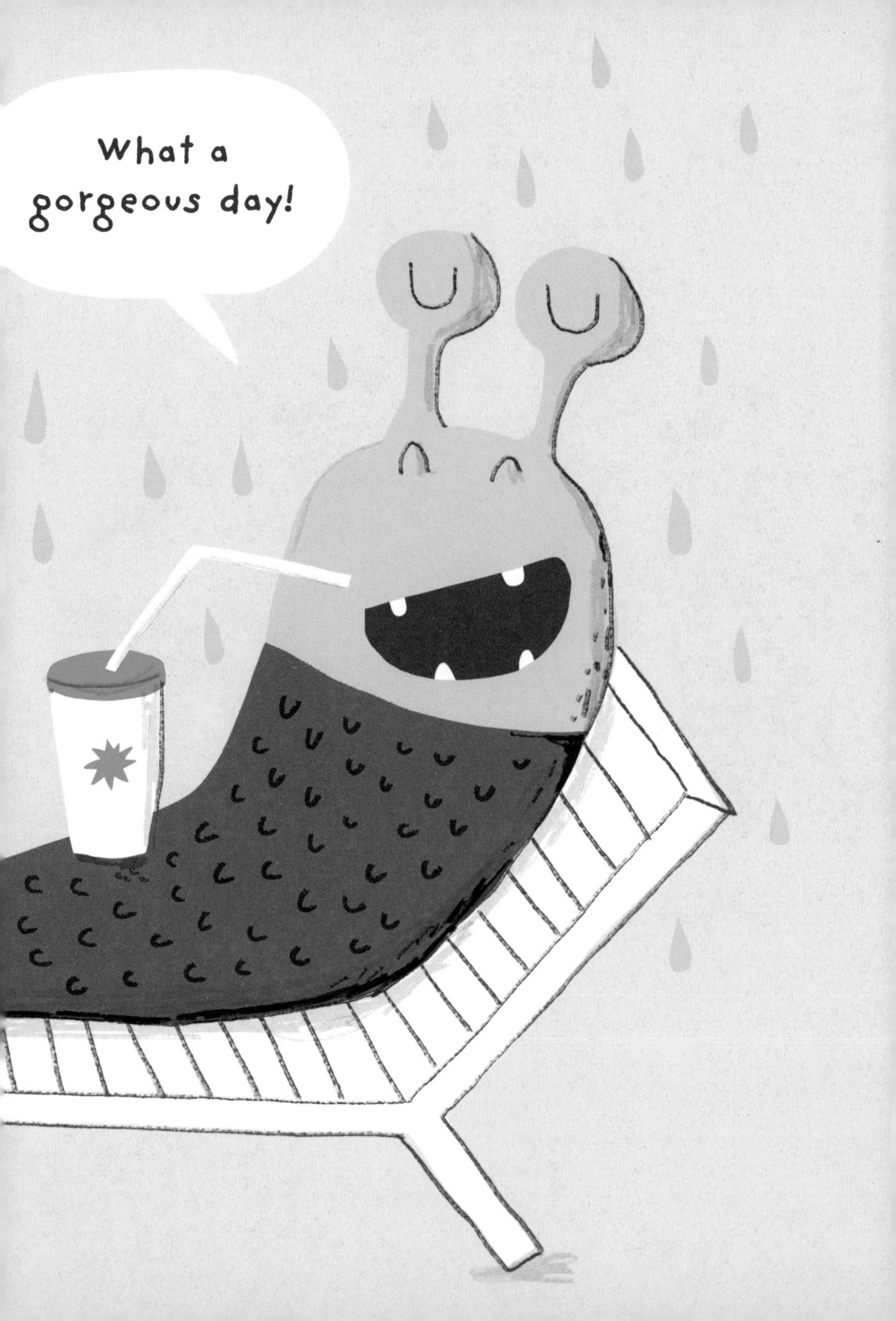
What a gorgeous day!

The mucus is very important because it helps the slug move by creating a

SLICK SURFACE.

It also acts like glue to help the slug climb up things like trees and walls.

What a HUGE slug!

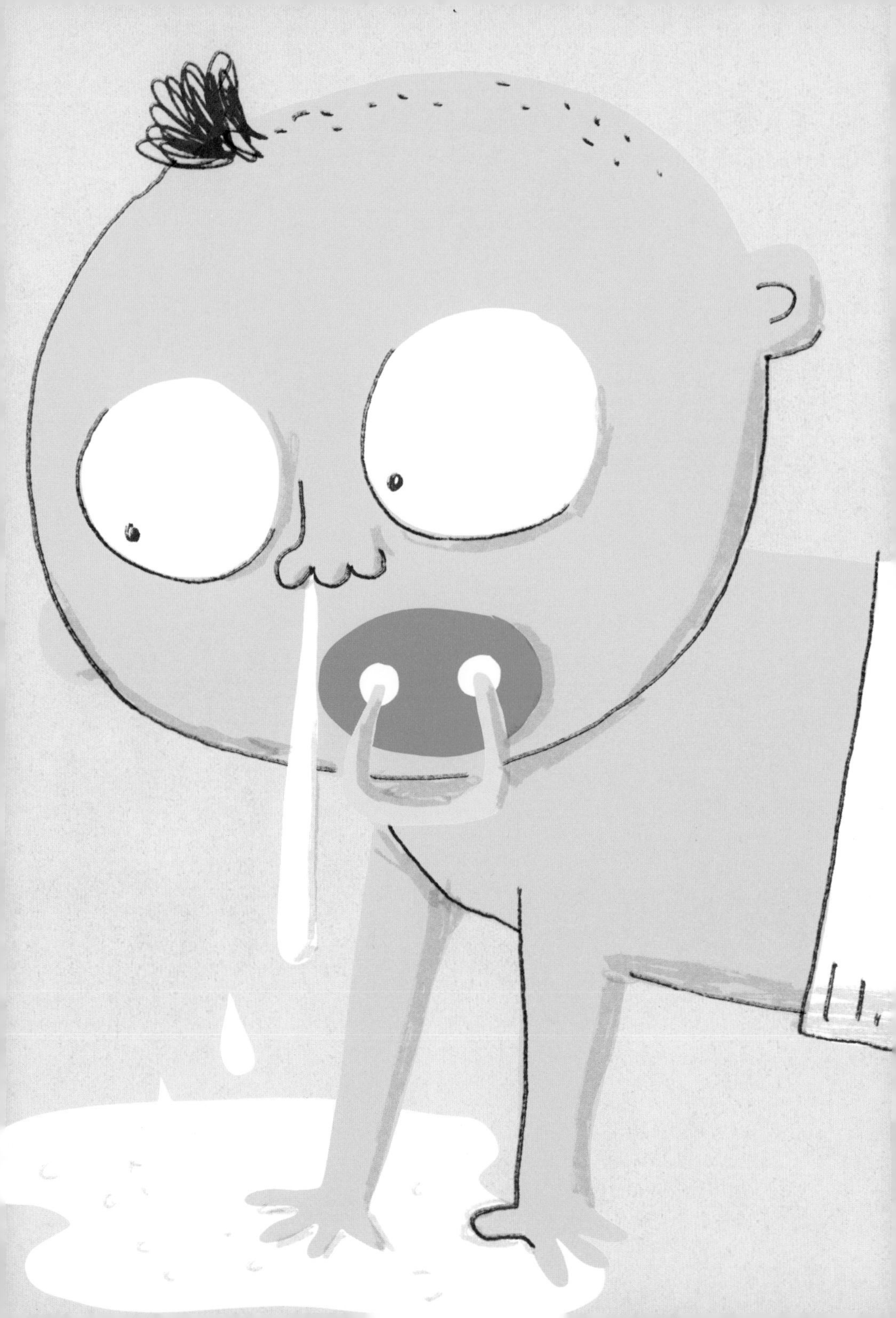

When it senses danger, the slug produces extra mucus so it becomes more

SLiPPERY

and can more easily escape its

PREDATORS.

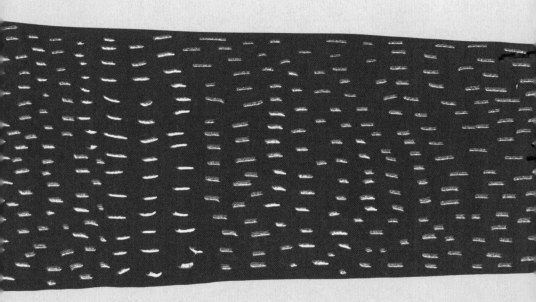

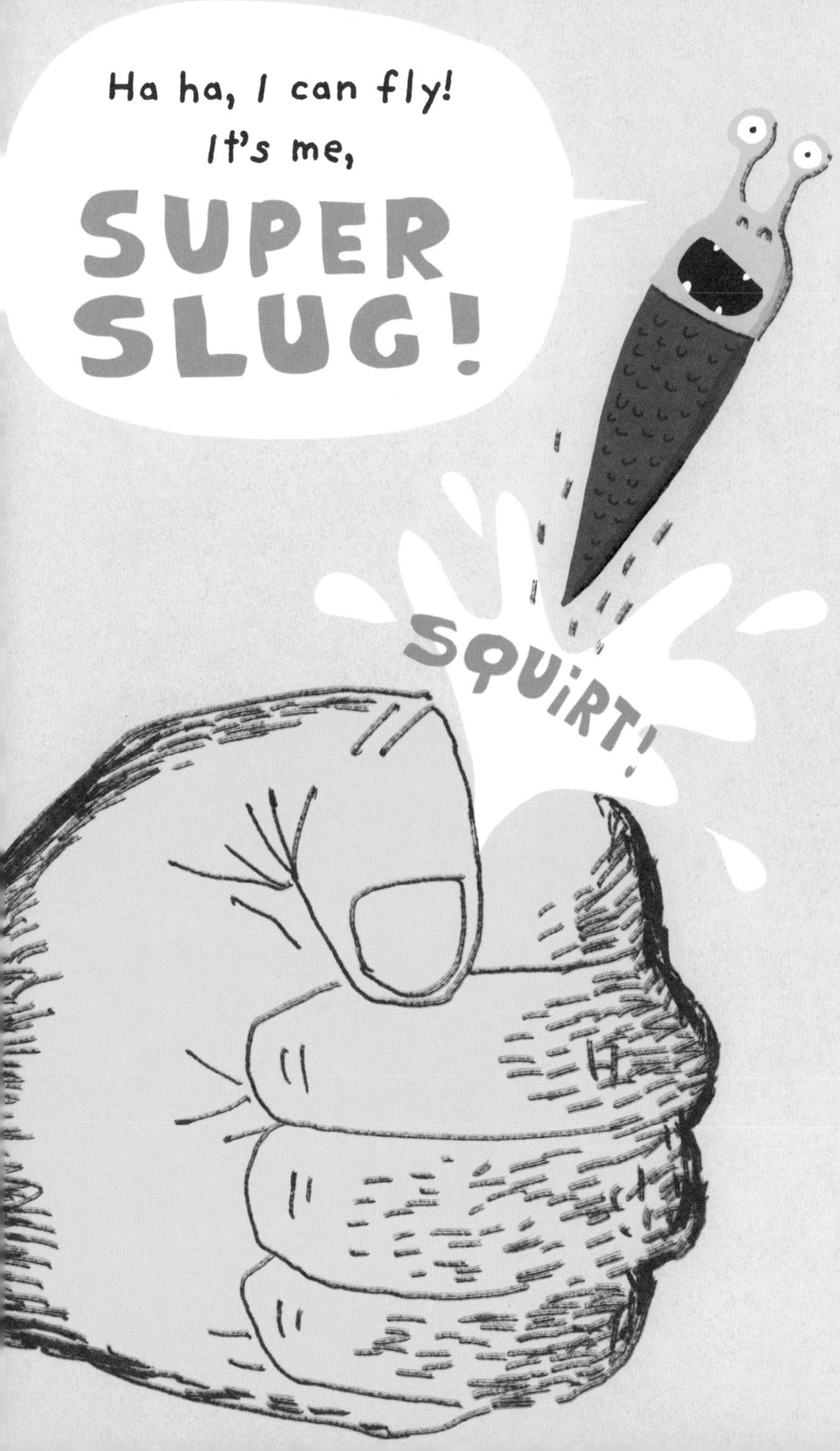
Ha ha, I can fly!
It's me,
SUPER
SLUG!
SQUIRT!

To find a

PARTNER

and have babies, the slug follows another slug's mucus trail.

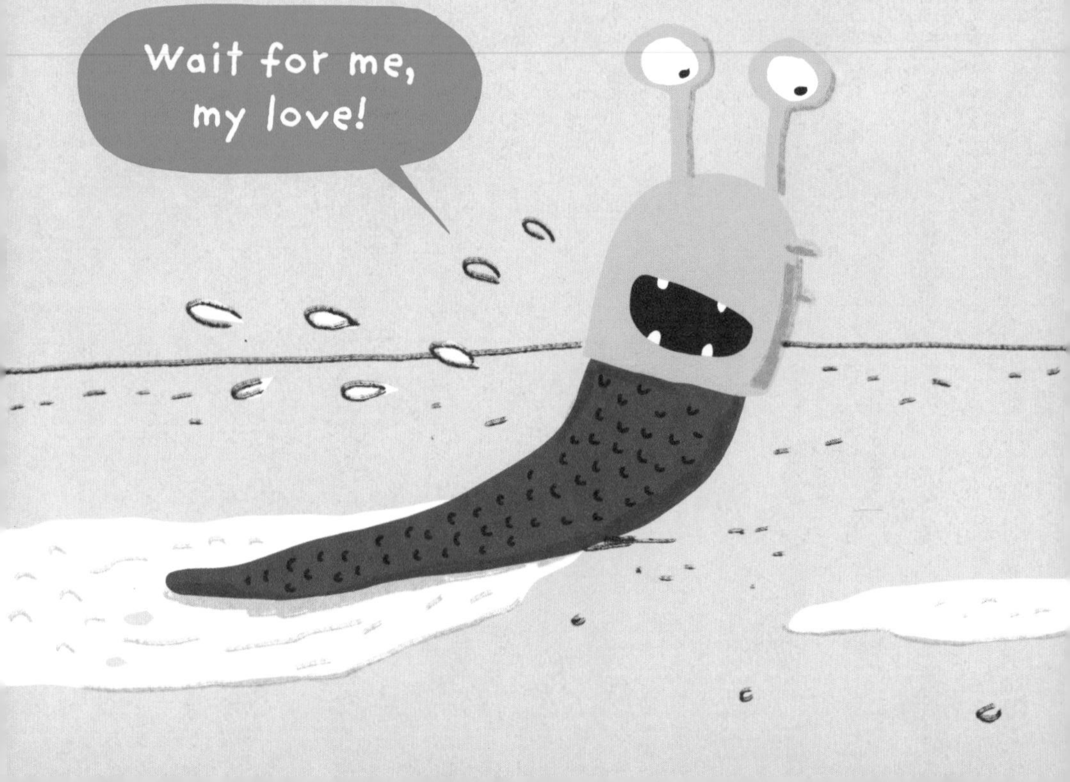
Wait for me, my love!

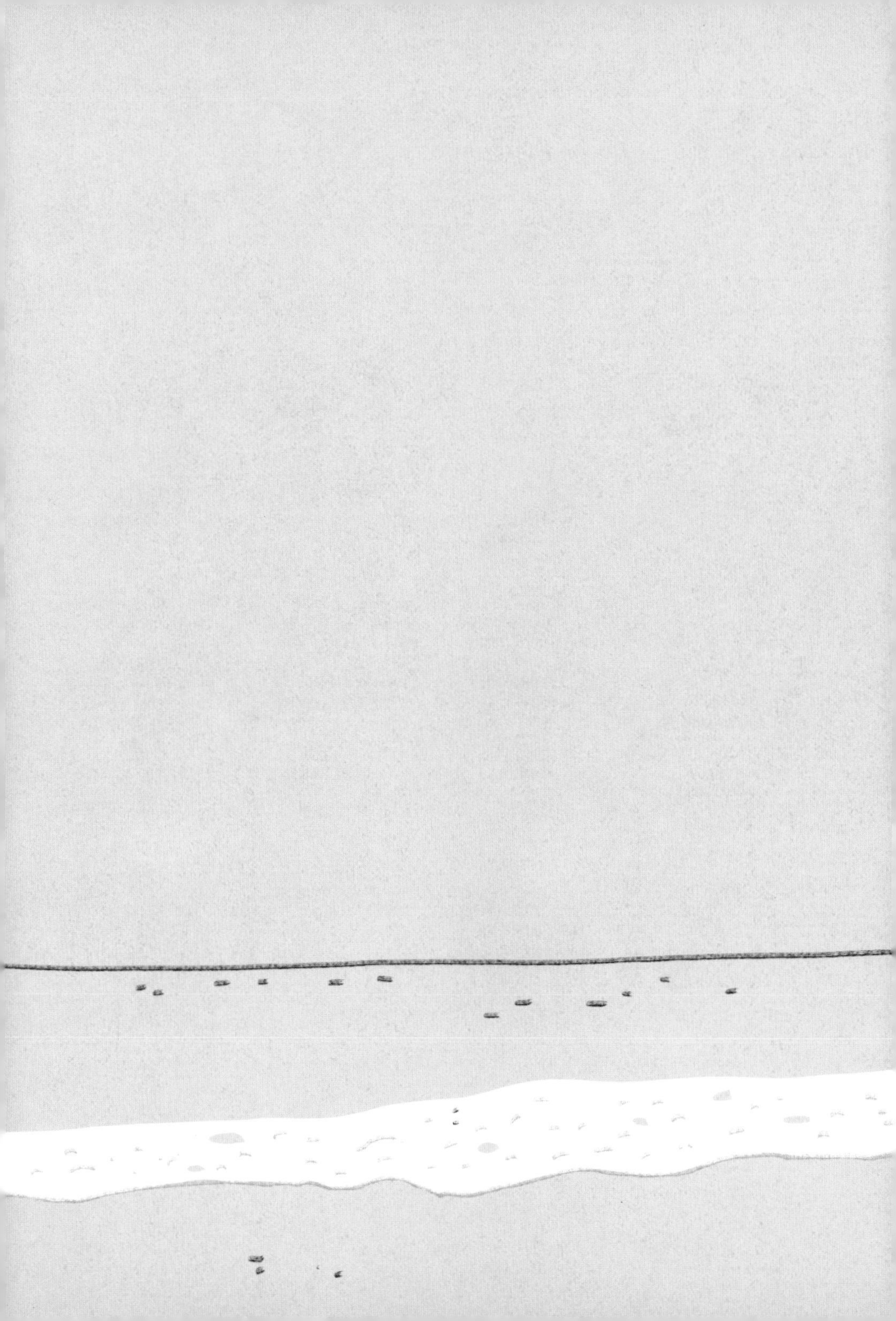

Just like the earthworm, the slug is male and female at the same time.

The slug lays its eggs in a hole in the ground or under a rock or piece of rotten wood.

BABY SLUGS,

tiny and transparent, will hatch in a few weeks.

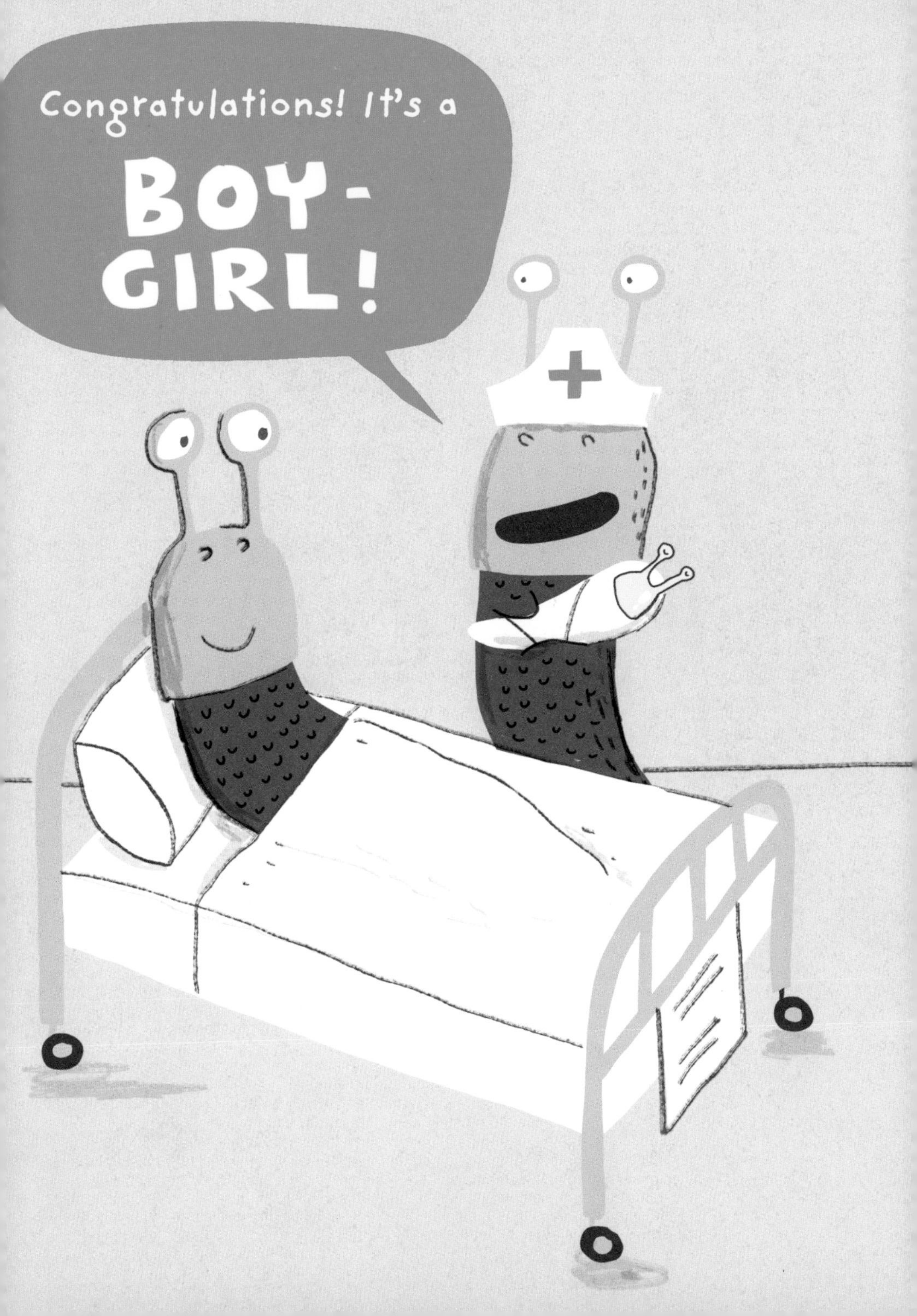
Congratulations! It's a BOY-GIRL!

The slug eats plants and mushrooms. Farmers and gardeners don't like slugs because they eat their

LETTUCE.

But slugs play an

iMPORTANT

role in the environment. They help to break down old or decaying plant and animal matter and turn it back into important nutrients for the soil.

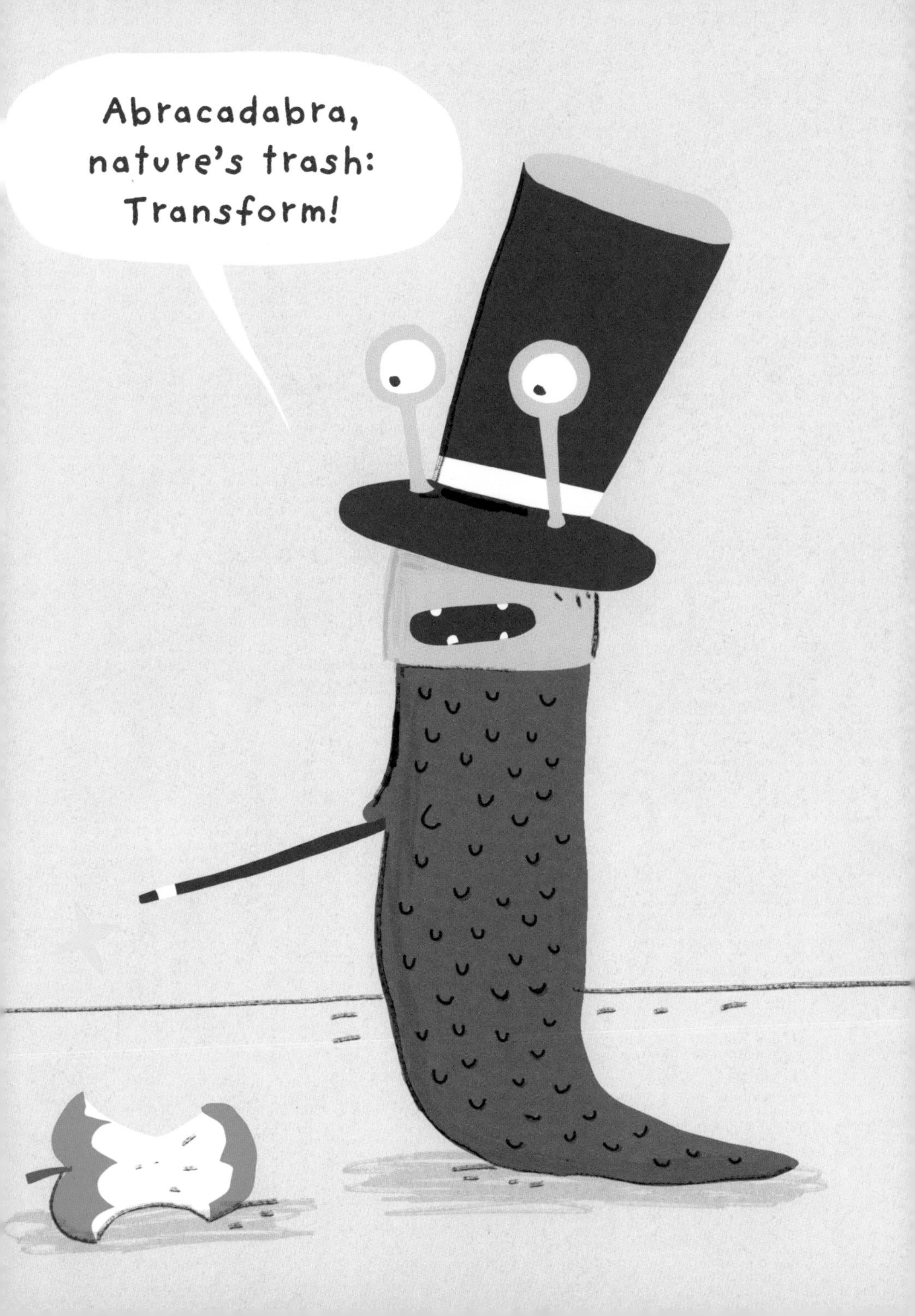
Abracadabra,
nature's trash:
Transform!

So next time you meet a slug, be nice.
Share some of your

SALAD

with it.

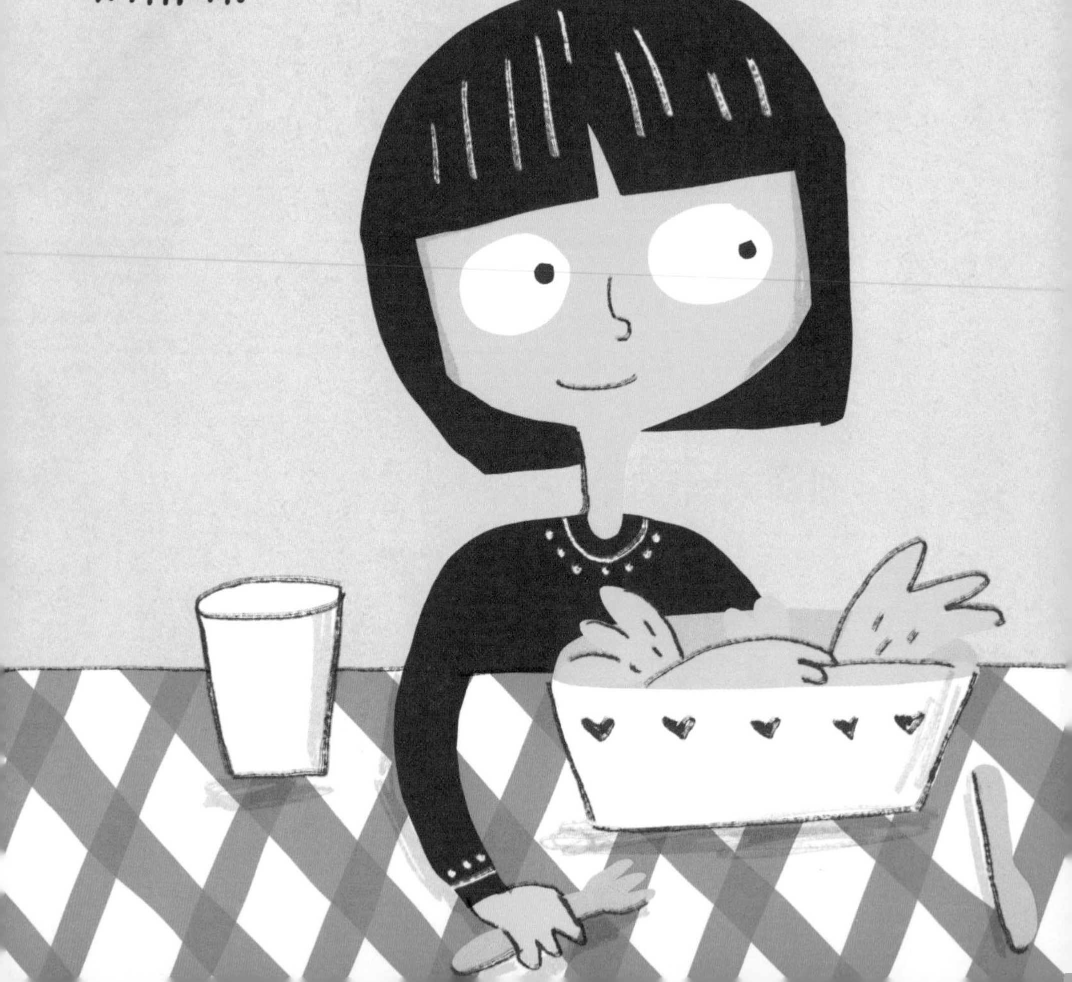

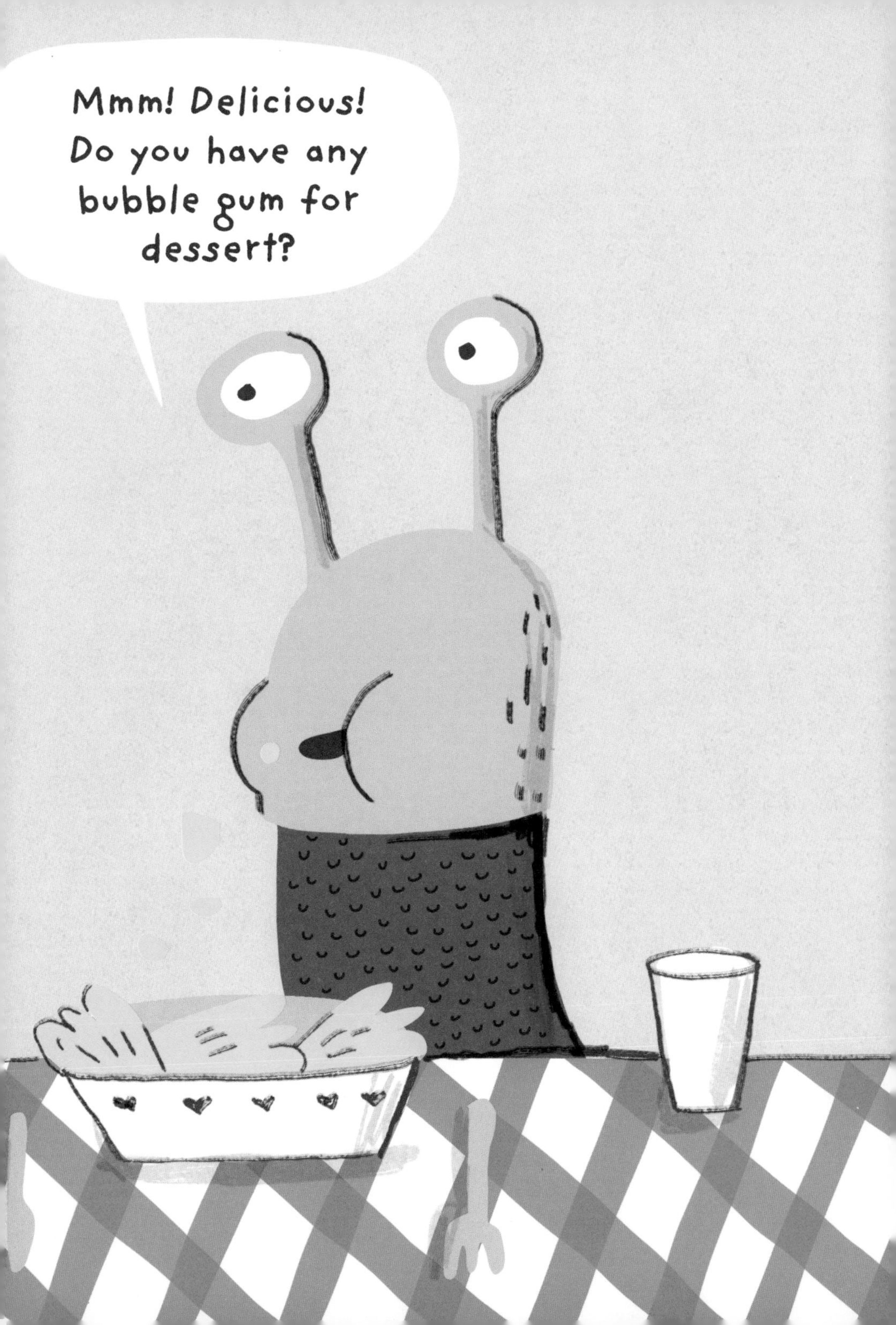
Mmm! Delicious! Do you have any bubble gum for dessert?

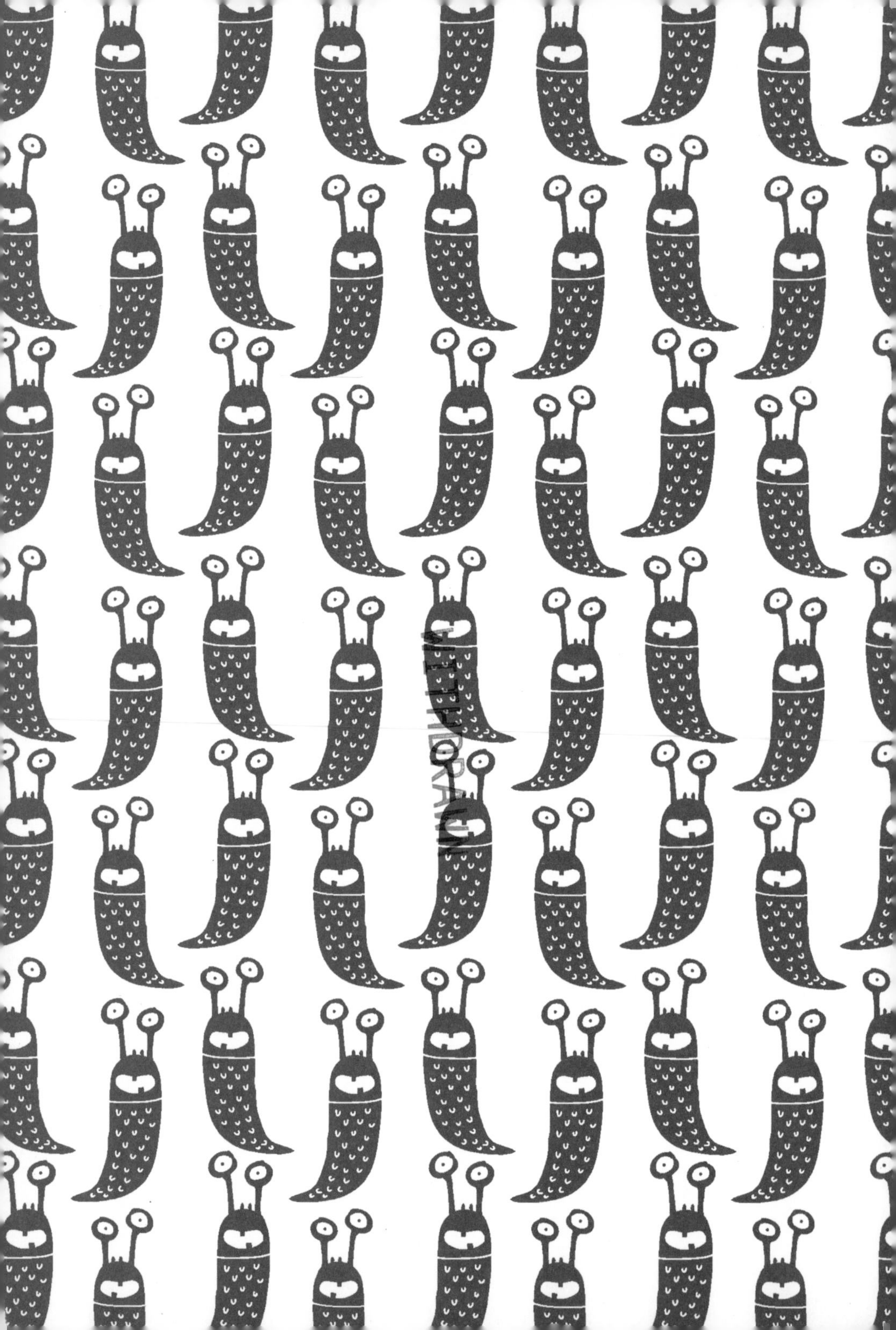